W9-AZG-565

Drinking Roses on Sunday

10,000 words to open the heart

By
Zach Beach

To contact the author, try the Internet.

1st edition.
ISBN-13: 978-1497489141
ISBN-10: 1497489148

Author Photo by Leah Colecchia, Share House Photography
Cover and Back design by Kajsa Hedman
Lovingly Edited by Caroline Smith, Ioana Tchoukleva, Christine Swayne

Zachary Beach
Emeryville, CA
www.zachbeach.com

now is the time for softness
now is the time for sweetness
now is the time for weakness

Drinking Roses on Sunday

Table of Contents

internal space

My question is,
who are you?

No really,
I must know,
who are you?

Who is this magnificent being I see smiling before me?
Such thoughtful eyes darting back and forth across the page.

I don't want your name,
silly,
that's just a few phonetics your parents assigned you
when you were born.

Who were you before your parents?
Who is carrying your corpse around?
Who is beating your heart?
What's beneath all that flesh and blood?

I know you've accomplished a lot.
But who are you right now?
In this moment?

Hmmm...
Maybe you don't know who you truly are.

In that case, let me tell you.

But first,

some elaboration is necessary…

for everything

This borrowed glob of atoms,
held so delicately together,
lets this thing I think is me,
flow through it for a short while.

There is peace in these mountains.
Every thing has a purpose,
and ours is to live, love, laugh, learn and let go,
but especially to love.

There is a special novelty in the way you smile,
like a log cabin in the woods with a spiral staircase.
So I carved a flower out of some leftover frosting,
when you asked me to pass the maple syrup,

I gave you two pieces of light and the palm of my hand.
Although I anticipate stormy weather,
these snowflakes couldn't be softer,
nor could my heart melt any faster.

My only wish is for my last breath to say: thank you.

tidal waves

We are dependent on everyone and everything around us.
Where would you be if your parents had never met?
Where would you be without the ground,
or the sun that feeds the same plants that nourish you,
giving oxygen and food and reasons to grow?

The order of the universe depends upon the atom.
So too does hate depend on the people that hold it.
Give no time to such ignorance,
replace it with kindness.
You cannot remove a burn,

but you can heal it from the inside,
give light no matter the darkness,
and reach out to one another,
like a spider spinning its first web,
with hope, promise and potential.

Rub up against these mountains.
Let's become glaciers in global warming,
running down Mount Vesuvius,
clearing forests, crushing cars,
drowning the Eiffel tower,

flooding the whole world with our love,
taking down authorities and empires and
anything
that stands in the way of love.
All you have is more than enough.

You are more heaven than earth,
more of a miracle in the making,
fluttering without wings,
a wind full of secrets
swooping up autumn leaves.

feel again

So we're all here trying to figure out what it means to be alive,
struggling to find emotional connection in a world of cubicles
          and studio apartments,
trying to dance with marbles in our shoes.

You smile on the street but no one bothers to look,
noses stuck in phones and flashing screens and Facebook,
hitting,
refresh,
      refresh,
               refresh.

Wishing for freshness anything really that'll make us feel again,
feel young again,
feel love again,
maybe this time,
     maybe this time,
              maybe this time,
time will not seem like a hit of a cigarette,
what
          a
             drag. . .
I want to write a status update that says:
Hey everyone,
I'll be gone for a few days or lifetimes.
While you're standing like pink flamingos,
I'll be staring into a wolf's eyes,
dancin' on egg shells,
sharing cups of coffee at airports,
running through train stations,
learning how to say goodbye,
asking the restaurant owner in Thailand if he catches his own
fish,
              (it doesn't matter I'm vegetarian anyways)
                             (yes that includes fish)

Oh!
And the sweet mangos in Guatemala are the best.
They always remind me of you.
I wonder if I'll ever get to tell you that,
And say,
hey,
        how have you been,
                it's been so long.
Yeah,
from way up here,
these city lights remind me of magic too.
I'm not sure why I ever left...
        Maybe I wanted to forget,
                just so I could remember you.

noble truths

The Buddhist teacher says life is suffering.
He says your paper airplanes will never fly as far as you want
and no matter how many people you surround yourself with
the demons of insecurity and loneliness could really care less.

But,
nature is neither silent nor noisy.
If you can feel the weight of a rose petal,
see the potential in the cocoon,
know the distance of an endless ocean,
notice the special kind of order in the way the vine
climbs up the wall and around the windows,
and give gratitude to the humble bumblebee
that makes much of life possible,

then,
you might know the true meaning of awe,
which is the surprising infusion
of cosmic significance into one's heart.
It is seeing the grandeur of life up close and personal,
and realizing you have the best seat in the house.

butterflies

Everything is love,
and love is everything.
Our job is to discover these truths,
again and again.

Your sweet heart,
is dripping with sugar.
You gave me caterpillars,
and plenty of time to change.

Said there is potential in empty space,
it is our duty to fill it up.
Much of this universe is cold and dark,
which is why your warmth couldn't be better,

which is why we hold hands as we walk
and we look outward,
to connect this feeling
and expand it into the world.

be patient

As a teenager,
I knew,
I wasn't the only one who thought about it.

Killing myself, that is.
Just jerk the steering wheel to the left into that oncoming semi,
that should do it.

Now many years later,
I know,
how fucking terrible that would have been.

I never would have fallen in love,
once, twice,
and a thousand more times.

So here are some things I've learned:
there is nothing more beautiful than the sound of a beating heart,
and sometimes there's nothing better than dancing.

And you can never watch the sunrise too many times.
Whether it's over Lake Michigan or through your bedroom
window,
the sun shines for you.

And the truth is,
the world needs you.
We need you.

I need you.
And if it doesn't feel that way now,
in a few years everything will be different.

And one day, while watching falling raindrops
leaving lightning-like trails down a window,
and squeezing the hand of a loved-one,

it will occur to you that
perhaps the most precious gift in the world
is that you're here to see it.

softly

I try to write words as gently as possible,
barely enough to leave a mark on the page.
So that as your eyes lightly glide along the curves of every letter,
a message flutters along your synapse,
negotiates its way through neurons,
ventures deeper than meaning and deeper still:
there is no need to wonder if you are loved,
you are the door to heaven and you also carry the key.

morning

I wake up.
It's cold.
There is frost on the window.
The sun hasn't risen yet.
Only the early early birds send soft calls to the morning.

This bed sheet isn't enough.
It’s too thin,
too short.
I shiver.

Ohhh,
but I turn over to find your back facing me,
sweet dreams are kissing your starry sleep.
I am drawn to you like a spaceship
back to the only living planet in the entire universe.
Your skin is soft like twilight,
I slip it on like a sweater out of the dryer.

Clouds form between my ears,
they drift with the wind.
My mind floats off towards
that dream
of a boy climbing trees
and picking apples out of his eyes;

you always were the sweetest one.

never give up on love

While it may not seem like much,
your body is a lighthouse.
You may run in circles searching for this and that,
but the divine light is inside you,
that's why there's so much brightness in the way you smile.

So smile.
Let the world know that you're there
and how much you'd be missed if you weren't.

Take care of this house.
Clean the windows every once in a while.
Drive for hours with no destination in mind
nor concern for return.
Let the road,
the night,
and the passing headlights
tickle your wanderlust.

Clear your mind,
trust the thoughts that arise.

Dare to follow your dreams,
never give up on love.

Buy a hammock.
Not the kind for your backyard,
the kind that folds into a light blue backpack
and gets carried through the woods on that trail
where you saw a mother deer that one time,

and you occasionally walk through a spiderweb.
It's ok,
don't worry,
it means there are some bumps on the road less travelled.

Bring sandwiches,
wear strong shoes,
see with your heart,
light your own way.

Find the open clearing where the oak trees
and sweet coneflowers gather before the sun,
where nothing is missing,
nothing is lacking,
nothing is left out,

and breathe.

stillness

Last night,
I left the house and walked out into the middle of winter.
As I folded my arms,
a shiver ran down my spine,
and I looked to the stars.

Each exhale
manifested ancestral ghosts
crossing the Bering straight,
covered in the skin of animals,
in a land before books and bullets,
where people actually looked out for each other.

Where the Gods cried crystal icicles,
covered the world in quiet cotton,
and let time be the artist of beauty.

With the silence penetrated by crackling campfires,
I thought,
perhaps *presence*
is an old friend
listening with a bit more understanding than your own.

express

My teacher said:
The greatest remorse is love unexpressed.

Since I always regret the things I don't do.
I stuck my heart in a helium balloon,
flew a kite to the top of the moon,
called you up there and said I couldn't see you too soon,
so we opened our hearts and made love all afternoon.

tingles

Find someone who puts needles under your skin,
lines up tingles down your spine,
plants Paris in your mind,
until a love story grows like a blossoming peach
becoming more and more vibrant with each kiss
and each sideways glance.

the source

Ok,
let me ask you this,
where does the rain come from?
Does it come from the sky?
Or does it come from the clouds?
Or the streams that flow through them?
Or does it come from years in the bottoms of oceans,
hitting rock bottom,
coming back to fall again?

Maybe that droplet,
breaking through the sky,
landing on your forehead,
sliding down your nose,
kissing your lips,
and falling to the earth,

came from a spring flower,
came from the tears of a broken heart,
came from forest fires and fireflies.

Maybe all raindrops came from the same place,
maybe they'll all return there too.

Ok,
let me ask you this,
where did you come from?
Did you come two-steppin' through that front door?
Or did you come from your mother's womb years ago?
Or did you come from a dream last night?
Or did you come back from years of searching the bottom of
    bottles,
hitting rock bottom,
coming back to live again?

Maybe that feeling,
breaking through our souls,
falling in love,
sliding through space,
kissing the stars,
and dancing on this earth,

came from the cosmos,
came from the tears of mother earth,
came from the fires of your ancestors.

Maybe we all came from the same place,
maybe we'll all return there too.

letters

Sometimes you have to write letters to yourself so that
later, when you can't stand the too big/too small of your
muscles/hips or that peeling skin around your dimpled chin
or those damn cheekbones that make your face look like—a
reminder comes in the mail and says: I don't know you but
one time I saw a sunset over a meadow in Yosemite cast
gorgeous fuchsian rays across the sky and it lit the clouds
on fire, well that was nothing compared to your touch and
kindness and the way your nose wrinkles when you're
thinking.
If there's one thing that keeps us all connected,
it's imperfection, we all want to follow our dreams but some
dreams you can only see out of the corner of your eyes and
dewdrops form in those same corners. Well it makes me sad
to think that the white tiger no longer exists in the wild and
to think that there is only one of you redefines the meaning
of preciousness. Please whatever you do, don't cut yourself,
and I don't mean just on the surface, I mean don't cut yourself
down, sell yourself short or picture your being as anything
less than the dancing wildness of pure ecstasy so momentarily
captured in a few layers of skin, polish, and beauty.

some thoughts

To me the world is no more solid than cotton candy,
sometimes walking feels a lot like floating,
something as simple as the soft summer breeze
reminds me to sing.

My dreams are far more real than the streetlamps
and morning fog.
I would not mistake the stars for infinity,
nor a yield sign for advice.

Although I could bounce
on beams of light,
I find myself sticking to immaterial things.
Like daydreams, or helium.

Yesterday's flypaper keeps
catching my buzzing thoughts.
I keep my heart on my short sleeve,
close enough for a whisper.

I feel life is underrated in terms of magic.
We can only possibly understand
a fraction of a grain of sand,
but in a hologram every piece contains the whole.

Maybe that's why eyes are the gateway to the soul.
Maybe that's why love is better than glitter and gold,
and anything else
you can hold in your hand.

city life

As I got off the subway train,
my headphones did little to block
the smell of piss, shit and body odor.
The homeless population seems to grow bigger every day.
The progress of society always leaves bodies behind,
sleeping on cardboard boxes in alley ways,
covered in those gray moving blankets,
dreams penetrated by the sounds of car horns and construction.

I catch the glance of a woman
looking a lot older than she is,
she's got raccoon eye shadow,
hair matted like a bird's nest,
face wrinkled like a rustled bed sheet.
She looks like she used to be a dancer,
she still wears the tutu and knee high socks
but no shoes this time.
I wonder if she too was young and alive
and had a whole lot of dreams.
Maybe she's living in a dream.
Maybe she still does dream
of being swooped up by an angel of light,
given a huge house and a sense of clarity,
a new outfit with some dancing shoes,
and a home-cooked meal with macaroni and ground beef,
her favorite.
Goddamn it's nice to be able to afford the cost of living.

You ever turn on the light and have it burn out just as quick?
I wonder what conditions caused it to spark out
at that specific time,
at that specific moment.

My friend turned schizophrenic at age 25.
He had no previous history

before falling off the precipice of mental sanity.
As god ripped out the pages of his memory,
he crumbled into the sidewalk cracks,
forever lost in the labyrinth of city streets.

You know those stories,
about people on their way to suicide,
but someone, somewhere
on the street,
sends them a smile and a wave,
and suddenly,
they change their mind?
So simple,
you don't need to be a doctor to save a life.

I wonder how close I am to the edge.
Sometimes I think I'd fall,
if I wasn't so held up by my loved ones.
So I try to lend a helping hand,
and say thank you to those that do.

trees

Deep down,
every poet knows
some things,
cannot be described,
for they are far too wonderful.
I could try for the rest of my life,

to express how much I like
to lightly glide my fingers
along the mountains of your back,
and how your goosebumps
feel like
little pieces of perfection.

The roots go down
as far as the tree goes up.
We dig into each other,
plant pieces of our hearts,
and love says:
grow.

Grow into each other,
and grow out into the world.
People will look
in awe at your beauty,
but only you will know
the true depth

and the soaking up of nourishment.
While it rains majesty on your leaves,
your teardrops will saturate mother earth,
only to be soaked up again,
through capillary action,
also known as,

with ease,
no effort at all,
just the same flow,
that keeps your lungs breathing,
that keeps you climbing higher and higher,
towards the music in the sky.

not really broken

My life is not a timeline.
I did not move from here to there.
More like a mosaic of broken glass:
each colorful shard set in the wet sands of time,
reflecting those around me,
piece by piece,
step by step,
sometimes sideways,
sometimes a few steps back.

I wished things developed like an old Polaroid picture,
slowly coming into focus.
Instead there were sad times and wrong directions,
bad luck and broken mirrors,
dark alleyways and a backpack of black cats;
I could have sworn this was the way.

My fingers are broken now,
from banging too hard on piano keys,
from holding on too tight to things
that have no time to stop and stay.

The story goes,
once upon a time,
there was a boy
who spent 50 years trying to see his own eyes,
who didn't realize that stained glass has character,
(you just have to let the light shine through it)
and that the folk singer in the dive bar may be the best show
you'll ever see,

and that if you want to make love to somebody,
you gotta start with the scars,
kiss them,
hold them,

like they're the stars.
Give extra care to the ones that you can't see,
the ones that go deep,
the ones that wake you up out of your sleep.

We all have sharp edges,
and we've all been hurt by them.
But if you put them all together,
like a broken glass mosaic
you'll see just how beautiful they fit.

where did the time go

Keep exploring,
there is always more to see.
Travel the world over,
let the wind scoop up your heart,
and set sail for the unknown.

But…
But…
recognize,
you will find yourself clutching old photographs,
sweeping up petals from dead flower arrangements,
returning home to find trees bigger than you remembered,
a field replaced with a Home Depot parking lot,
and lovers drifting away to friends and friends to strangers.

Google image search "melancholy"
and you will find bare trees weeping raindrops,
fog covered lakes with an eerie calm,
hands pressed against cold window panes,
the moon setting behind trees on the horizon,

and blue, blue, blue.
Like a shadow cast by fading memories that asks,
where are the billions that breathed this air 150 years ago?
Where does the sound of the church bells go?
What about that special feeling you had
with that special someone?

Kiss your mother.
Hug an old friend.
Nostalgia,
like life,
is a mixture of pleasure and sadness.

There’s a reason why half of all people believe in ghosts,
it’s comforting to fool ourselves into thinking
what will never be again is still here.

phases

Jump.

A child stands at the edge of a diving board,
not two feet above water.
He's nervous. He looks down.
He doesn't know how deep the water goes,

but he's pretty sure it could swallow him up
without even chewing.
He looks around for reassurance.
His mother, with bug-eyed sunglasses,

and a wide brimmed hat,
is engrossed in a self-help book
that won't change a damn thing in her life.
He's on his own now.

He takes a deep breath,
holds it in with puffed cheeks,
plugs both nostrils with one hand,
and learns to fly.

Fall.

They've been going out for years.
Still every time her eyes catch his,
his heart wobbles like a dubstep track,
his feet feel lighter than air.

This time he says,
I want your skin pressed up against mine,
and I want to hold you closer than that.
I want 75 years and one night with you.

I want to watch water droplets

run down the curves of your skin in a candlelit bathtub.
She asks him if he's serious, if he means the things he says
and, to be honest, he's not even sure,

his voice wobbles like his heart.
But there's magic in the way she moves,
there is sweetness in her smile,
he wants to dance across those upturned lips.

He picks her up, tosses her
onto the bed of freshly cleaned sheets and down pillows,
looks around,
and dives in.

Float.

Two old men are playing chess in a park
underneath a cherry blossom tree.
One of them,
eyes frantically shifting back and forth,

looks up from the board and asks,
"It's all going to be over soon, huh?"
The other man replies,
"Yep. It's only a matter of time now."

"Can I get a do-over?" the man asks.
"Sorry, no takebacks," the other man replies.

The man looks around.
He takes in the birds,
the mothers pushing strollers,
the taxi cabs in traffic slowly passing by,

and the streams of warm water
cascading down the fountain in the center.
The man closes his eyes

and directs his face towards the sun.

Suddenly, the cherry blossom tree wakes up
and shakes its branches,
causing petals to flutter and fall,
like the sands of time.

As the color pink gathers around the table and chairs,
the tree reaches down,
scoops up the old men
and they burst into autumn leaves.

for anis

I will fall asleep tonight,
thinking lightly of poetry and feathers,
passing prose through prisms,

dreaming of dandelions plucked into a bouquet,
handed to the teacher in a half-washed pickle jar,
and accepted graciously,
because love does not say no.

or today

If I die tomorrow,
there's one thing I will say,
that every moment was beautiful,
I cherished every day.

The people made it worth it,
and all the love I received,
filled me to wholeness,
and put my heart at ease.

oh you

You
are the astonishing,
altogether unbelievable,
almost unfathomable,
abounding in amazement,
child of the universe.

The inspiring integration of
atoms, salt, cells, history and sun,
and a whole lot of empty space,
so much that there's room in your heart for Mount Everest
and all of Mother Earth's children.

To cut through such complexity,
try herbal tea and a bay window,
try watching the geese take rest from flying south,
try feeling the morning fog,
try riding the sound of the sitar,
try dancing like James Brown,
try weaving your own cloth.

Some knowledge can only be lived, not learned.

Now stop striving,
give up on trying to achieve anything at all,
see if you can sit still.
Notice how life has you completely surrounded,
how love emanates from everything.

How the tireless work of a few million generations of ancestors,
has resulted in where you are today,
and they are happy
that you're here.

Gratitude in a breath.

open here

In our mind lives picture frames around fragile concepts
and other things that break with time.
There are also judgments,
thoughts of war and death,
your mother's recipe for broccoli cream soup,
plain explanations and great expectations.

But in our heart there lies:
a library of mystery books,
a red neon sign flashing
[open] ...
[open] ...
[open] ...
watercolors and string strewn about
with neither rhyme nor reason,
a cacophony of unintelligibles,
and plenty of room for the unknowables.

When life shoves me into the shadows,
I hear a voice from there that says
yes,
yes this too has a lesson in it.
Sorrow, pain, despair.
There is a space for everyone,
to sit,
to rest,
to tell their story little by little
until it's over,
like the clouds disappearing
so the stars may peak through.

on second thought

I was thinking to myself
waving my hand in the air,
what's between the atoms?
What else is there?

What is the weight of a moment?
Or a thought?
What makes a poem?
Can science prove one exists?

What would it be like to throw a paper airplane on the moon?
How far would it go?
I imagine, the lack of air resistance coupled with just a quarter of the gravitational force found on earth,
an airplane thrown upward at 45 degrees from atop the crater that forms the right eye of the man on the moon would clearly go—

"Where does belly button lint come from?"
She questioned,
holding the culprit between thumb and forefinger.
"How come you have so much?"

I turned over in bed.
"Honey, you're interrupting my sweet reverie."

"Oh yeah, Mr. Rilke?
What were you thinking about this time?
How the light from the sun has travelled for eight minutes and twenty seconds at six-hundred-and-seventy-million miles-an-hour to the Earth just so you could see yourself pee in the morning?
I got some news for you Sir Walter Raleigh,
life is happening right here,"
she said, taking my hands and placing them on her breasts.
They were soft like the feeling you get when your friend is confiding in you the secret traumas of his childhood,

soft like snowflakes landing on your tongue,
like I was holding the cumulus clouds above Cleopatra's head
like--
"Cut it out!"
She said,
"I'm here with you so
I can be here with you so
you'd better be here with me.
And while this whole universe disappears and reappears a trillion times a second
it's Love that holds it all together.
And love is universal in a life-everlasting-wreathing-through-the-cosmos kind of way but
it's also more personal than the stink in your shoes.
So if William Blake can find infinity in a grain of sand
then you damn well better be able to see the world in your belly button."

my advice

Live in such a way
to challenge people’s assumptions and judgments.
Understand others' opinions but pay no mind to them.

Listen to the things that move you.
Kind of like music,
but more like maybe you’ve been a violin string your whole life
and just need to let the world rub up on you a little harder,
and your footsteps will begin
to look like a melody of quarter notes
strewn across power lines and floating off into the horizon.

Build a shrine for peace.
Walk outside,
see no difference between people.
We all want happiness,
we all want to feel alive and know what it means to be so.

Have sex and laugh about it.
Pluck out one of your hairs and give it to the wind.
Maybe that’s all we are to the world and maybe that’s
all we need to be:
human, free, and seen only by how well
the light passes through us.

relax

As little drops of rain
gather on a leaf outside my window,
they pool together,
until until,
it's too much.

But the leaf doesn't break,
it sighs, it relaxes, it lets go,
just enough to bounce back.
Sometimes flexibility is a sign of resilience,
and giving out is a way of protection.

Sometimes you need to fly north
to the cold winters of your own fears,
tear away layers,
shed hardened skin,
and laugh yourself silly,

until a song of tender kisses,
gently nibbles on your ears,
and the beauty of your own being,
slowly eats away at self-judgment.
And the tears of happiness gently pool,

in the leaf of your own heart,
and surrender becomes more than a word,
it defines what falling in love really means,
and for once you smile at the universe,
while the stars smile back.

paper planes

Oh right,
I was supposed to tell you who you are.
Let me see if I can explain.

If you were made out of paper,
your being would be folded into a heart-shaped envelope.

Inside would be all the stories of the world:
the mother breastfeeding her baby at the bus stop in Mexico,
the hookah smokers in Turkey,
Russian children playing with toy cars,
a Buddhist monk sweeping the floor in Tibet,
the call to prayer waking up devotees in Iran,
prostitutes in Hong Kong at 5 am
looking for their last trick of the night,
and the tai chi master beginning his morning practice.

All of these
are wrapped up inside you.

All of life flows through you.

that art thou

Wherever you are,
don't wait for anything.
In waiting for the next moment,
we miss the current one.

In wishing for tomorrow,
we miss the dream of today.
Meet right now like an old friend you haven’t seen in years,
like the answer is right before you and has been there all along.

Find constant contact with each experience,
fall in love with the beauty of your own soul,
like your name is more than just significant,
like life is soaked into your pores.

Don’t let negativity burden you,
for there is no room nor time
for judgment or ill-will
in the grand scheme of things.

Mistakes sure,
but those are like dandelions in an open field,
they too have their place,
let them be.

They say that light,
has both particle and wave properties.
They say that
it is both and neither and something else altogether.

Well,
you are both human and spirit
and neither and something else altogether indescribable.
Don’t let anyone tell you otherwise.

new endings to old beginnings

I got lights in my shoes.
Meaning that light carries my feet.
Meaning that,
meaning carries me through.

Now,
the thing about light is,
it's a process,
a continuous movement.
Just as quickly as a photon passes it disappears.
And like a river,
light also needs a source.

So when they say,
you are light
or
you are divine,
they really mean,
you are the source of everything.

When I asked a Buddhist monk,
why they repeated mantras so much,
he said,
"Well,
things have a funny way of coming around, ya know.
Day turns to night turns to day.
Life turns to death turns to life.
Everything arises and passes,
arises and passes,
arises and passes.

Om Aim Saraswati namaha
Om Aim Saraswati namaha
Om Aim Saraswati namaha

Saraswati is our river goddess.
Like light, a river also needs a source.

So you must take the story full circle.
You must take yourself full circle.
Do not cease from this exploration.*
Because things have a funny way of coming around, ya know.

If you look deep enough within
you'll fine new endings to old beginnings,
like planting gardens on gravesites.

The truth is:
the source and the flow
are the same thing
and everything
that there is."

*
We shall not cease from exploration,
and the end of all our exploring
will be to arrive where we started
and know the place for the first time.
- T. S. Eliot

create life in life

My advice is this:
go have sex in the woods.
Right now.
Don't delay.
While it my seem like an easy task,
so easy in fact you can put it off for tomorrow,
or next weekend, or next month or never,
really it is quite difficult.
Some people go their wholes lives without even trying it.
You must get away from the city,
the people, the obligations,
you must turn away from this.
Somewhere between the couch cushions
and insurance commercials,
you must make time for yourself.

For love,
it's a long drive.

When you get to the national forest,
park your car on the side road past the main entrance.
Bring a blanket and head towards the rising sun.
Pass over the hill where the sound of crunching leaves
under your feet sounds sweeter than Mozart.
After the owl's nest on the second hill,
it will dawn on you that
the world is better when left behind.

And perfection is the experience of having nothing
and realizing
you are everything.

draw me

Draw me a picture of passion,
draw me in.

Let’s peel onions,
shed layers of clothing and inhibition,
walk on white sand beaches,
swim in the crystal blue waters of your eyes.

Let’s read palms,
speak body language,
discover what they mean when they say,
anything is possible.

Ever watch a helium balloon float off into the sky and wonder
if it will ever touch ground?
I find love is kind of like that.
Rising into wordlessness,
finding intensity in everything.

tell it again

Last night I fell asleep with the window open.
Let the city sounds enter my dreams:
sirens in the grotto,
car honks in the forest,
subway trains and taxis moving knights and peasants
around a great whimsical kingdom
with crosswalks, coffee shops and gunshots,
and homeless trolls living under the state street bridge.
I heard that Rapunzel took the fire escape
and Humpty Dumpty was rushed to the Emergency Room.

It may be dangerous to go out at night alone,
but on a noble quest with a sword in the shape of an umbrella
and a magic pouch with your wallet and keys,
the city lights align in your favor.

Life is a grand adventure or nothing.
It is itself the point:
a story of bewilderment
to be told,
to be heard,
to be experienced again and again,
discovering something new each time.

bienvenue

This is the world,
sights, smells, sounds and all.
Welcome.
Everything has already been laid out.
Paris is nice, if you can make it,
if not, a bench, a park, a pond, and a kiss will do.

I know,
it's like you just arrived,
and in a blink of an eye you'll be gone.

Here's the trick of it:
you cannot get a one-up on life,
you cannot stand above it,
you are inextricably,
undeniably part of it
and part in it.

So let go and throw your heart,
your art,
and yourself into the storm dear child.
You are a gift full of gifts.

you can never have too much

How do I put this delicately?

I want me,
you,
and a bottle of lube.

scissors

You so sexy like,
I've never been so wet like,
your paper beats my rock like,
you make me sing show tunes like,
you folded my brain into an origami swan like,
I'm not sure if there is even a problem,
but the solution is cuddles.

buoyancy

When there is broken glass on the floor,
and the ground beneath your feet is crumbling
like you knew that it would,
and the lessons of impermanence and letting go,
are disguised as grief ripping our your soul,

know that the average cloud weighs a million pounds,
which means no matter how heavy your heart is,
or how heavy the world seems,
it can still float.

Your life
begins when
you realize
you only have one.

Today's mantra is:
I'm here to love
I'm here to love
I'm here to love

interlace

Join me.
Lay here in the grass like gravity has tripled,
(surrender)
release imagination from its cage,
let the cool breeze dance with your hair.
There is nothing to seek after,
when the world is coming right for you.
Be still, until everything explodes:
your love,
your life,
and a spirit that calls:
join me.

croissants

I discovered some wishes in my cereal bowl.
My spoon carried them slowly up to my lips.
Trembling,
I examined them a bit closer
and found:

a million dollars and a drum set,
the rain disappearing right now,
me playing the guitar really well,
also me being appreciated for who I am,
and pants being more comfortable.

It's always funny to me,
how you pronounce *croissant*,
and how full hearts are lighter than empty ones,
and life is a poem that never ends.
We must write it in spite of everything.

Your blood renews itself every 120 days.
Cells break apart and are born again a thousand times a second,
so you,
so you can look up towards the sky,
see this life spiral continue up into infinity.

The word heaven is so close to haven,
I want to remix the bible so that
the choir sings uninterrupted interludes for breakfast,
God is melting butter into warm wheat toast,
and peace is so delicately placed in all our hearts.

warming up

I was born under the February full snow moon.
My mother looked into my newborn eyes and said,

"You brighten my heart,
a scented flower lightens the air anywhere,

may you go out into the world,
wherever the wind takes you.

Poke fun at the sky,
breathe in my love.

We don't smile for ourselves
but for others to see."

Much later I decided that
a hopeless romantic

is somebody who desires love
but does not believe that they deserve it.

There are those that find the thing they want
but self-sabotage and fear keeps it in the shadows.

There's no one. No one.
No one more deserving of love on this earth than you.

I know this because
the bus stop is cold,

and watching the cars go by is even colder,
but your eyes are wide open,

deep and knowing.
Cupping those bare shaking hands together,

you breath out the love of pure being,
always warming, always there.

simply a measurement of change

Time is mostly an illusion,
not much more than a mental concept.

I've seen children with more wisdom than their grandparents.
My little cousin said,
"You know mister,
you can say what it is you have to say
without being mean,"
after I yelled at him for climbing too high up a tree.
"Kids are made for exploring!" he countered,
climbing higher.

And I've seen an elderly couple hop into a red convertible,
smack each other a kiss and gun it for Sunset Boulevard.

We've all had an hour of class go on forever
and the same day happen again and again,
and when you spent all night talking with your future spouse
but it only felt like 5 minutes you'll look back on that moment
and say,
that's when I knew.

So I call my friend "the magician with cancer"
because he turned 6 months to live into
15 years,
3 kids,
2 graduations,
and 1 reason to:
live your own life and not what others expect of you,
speak like it's the last words you'll ever say,
and oh so tenderly bring hope into the soft belly of your being.

anything?

When cardiac arrest sent my father to the hospital,
I learned the fear of uncertainty,
the same way a passenger grips the airline chair,
when the plane bounces upon landing.

The doctor at the emergency room told me,
"Well,
anything can happen to anybody at anytime.
Someone perfectly young and healthy

can come in with a pain in their chest,
and never end up leaving.
Another woman down the hall is battling lung cancer
although she's never smoked a cigarette in her life.

Life is scary but it's also amazing,
in these walls people leave this world
and new ones enter it,
in the meantime, being human is not easy.

We all hope for the best."

choose love

When your son crashes the family car,
the one you spent half your salary on,
but goddamn he made it out alive,
choose love.

When forgiveness comes knocking on your front door,
but the doorknob is too hot to handle and
you've been burned enough,
see that you deserve more than a few thousand diamond rings,
and choose love.

When the heat of anger boils over,
and you get so mad you could just—
find rest in the soft clouds of your own heart,
and choose love.

When grief turns into a crashing tidal wave,
threatening to take you down with it,
hold those that are close to you even closer,
and choose love.

When failure is too close for comfort,
and no one questions your abilities more than you do,
tune into the vibrations of the YOUniverse
coursing through those veins,
and choose love.

When for some crazy reason or any reason at all
you can't stand yourself,
and you want to bang your head a few times on a brick wall
until your brains fall out,
try coloring that gray matter with a little pink and blue,
and choose love.

When that boy doesn't call you back again,

and your heart feels like it's splattered across a car windshield,
let the tightness in your chest explode into a million violet petals,
and choose love.

Sometimes when something is broken,
you have to break it even further,
to put the pieces back together.

And sometimes,
the gods envy you,
because you can hold your breath
and create joys that fly over mountains,
like a good piano song,
or a sparkle in someone's eye.

metta

You,
are beyond beautiful.
Your face glows in the dark,
your eyes reflect who I want to be.
I bow down to your amazing grace,
my forehead on the ground,
Mother Earth tells me she is proud of you,
and how you walk upon her.

How are you such a dream?
How did I get so lucky?
Am I worth it?
Aren't my imperfections too many?
Is this feeling of fragility more than an illusion?

You reply,
"The river is not bothered by the rocks,
the same wind resistance that slows down the plane also lifts it up,
and love is a gentle rain.
It does not pick here but not here.
When I say I love you,
I mean,
I love all of you."

anytime is a good time

I like accidentally exchanging things with you,
how a few pairs of my underwear are now in your bottom drawer,
and I've been meaning to give you back those earrings you left,
and the poetry book you gave me,
and that jar of coconut oil,
and a deep sense of special.

For breakfast
we eat everything bagels,
and mobius bacon strips,
capture light years through time-lapse,
while sushi rolls off your salmon colored lips,
you nibble on my peach fuzz,
lick the sweat off my cheek,
and tell me it tastes like miso soup.

You light up my kaleidoscope dreams,
turn everything acoustic,
sleep in the shape of a good book
lit by a firefly lantern.

I have heard that
even a black sand beach in Iceland
is a good place for hearts to touch.
Because seeing yourself at the cusp of infinity,
while wispy grey skies,
an ocean of cold emptiness
and a colder breeze makes your eyes water,
radiance is still a state of mind,
and love only needs you to thrive.

the doors

I watch as the smoke of nag champa
dances with the air,
it moves with more grace
than the world's greatest ballerina.

The hippy in tie-dye tells me I should take LSD,
he says there's more to reality,
than what meets the eye.
At least we can both agree on something.

I too want to tear the bandage off,
(or maybe it's a blindfold)
jump through the doors of perception,
watch in amazement as the ladybug munches on leaves,
opens its wings with trepidation,
and leaps into the unknown.

We live a mystery,
the destination is never clear.
I have no idea "what I'm doing with my life" either,
I tuck my trust in between the waves of emotion,
where we dream and dance together.

Like this candle flame,
first there was nothing
and then there was you.
Just like that.

The Universe is,
while everything simply changes forms,
a few seconds later the river is not the same.
So tomorrow,

we'll meet each other again,
and again,

find truth in each other’s smiles,
and love in each other’s eyes.

hear that?

All my life,
I have tried to practice listening.
My advice is,
start with the easy stuff.

Like the birds welcoming the morning,
or the bubbling of coffee brewing,
or the cackle of eggs hitting the frying pan.
For the sweetest music is not played by instruments.

Then go deeper into the challenge of life,
listen to your own sadness,
understand what it has to say,
those tears may be your greatest teacher.

Place one ear on the breast of a loved one,
find the same heartbeat that keeps us all alive,
feel the rise and fall and rise and fall of the breath,
exchanging thanks with the world around us.

Lend the other ear to silence,
feel the nature of your own being,
a peaceful place of pure potentiality.
Fall asleep and don't forget to dream.

fill me up

I wanted everything,
so I fell in love,
with life, with my own breath,
with you,
and you and you and you.

I, just a small pond,
but gratitude, the waterfall,
flowing in,
filling up,
overflowing into the green earth,
growing flowers and trees and
refracting light into the darkest of places.

life's riches

The rich man has more,
wants more.

The content man has some,
is content with some.

The wise man has nothing,
wants nothing.
Deep down he knows,
he is part of everything.

paris

Let's build a house of memories.
Fill it with love.
Let our family and friends come visit.
We'll show them how we named our sunroom Paris.
So we could say,
let's go have breakfast in Paris.
And when everyone leaves,
you say, I want to fuck you in Paris.

Our backyard will be an open prairie,
where pollen floats in the wind,
and dragonflies swirl in figure 8s,
and maybe once in a lifetime a butterfly
lands softly on your pinky finger--
careful,
don't move,
breathe and it's gone.
Some moments are like that.
After that, I started calling you Special.

You started calling me Peanut Butter Cup,
and told me,
"The world is much more beautiful than people think,
and you are capable of so much more
than your mind can imagine.
But you have to let go.
This is not a test,
you cannot save it for later.
You must jump in the deep end,
go swimming with vulnerability.
Find your feelings and the courage to express them.
Let me love you.
Let me in.
Your heart does not need protection.
(Your dick does)

Remember that night
you read my body like a map,
fingers tracing each and every curve,
crisscrossing mountains and valleys,
with more fascination and curiosity then even the most intrepid explorer?
Keep that feeling close.
So no matter how many years
and fights and breakups and makeups,
you still remember Paris."

in loving memory of brian baker

As your tears waterfall down,
let them combine into the pool of all the tears wept before,
you are not alone in this.

When the world consumes you in sadness,
and leaves you in the cold,
let love wrap you up like a child,
you are not alone in this.

We both know pain now.
We both need to take more chances,
give more light,
savor every smile,
cherish every moment.
And please,
open your heart,
take everything in.
If you do,
then nothing will be left behind.

this is the new year

This is the new year.
I'm crashing champagne bottles on cruise ships.
My resolution is to
fall in love with everyone
and everything I've ever touched,
tell secrets until I'm running on empty,
until the scabs come off,
the scars shrivel away,
and all I'm left with is a
heart that drips in watercolor,
and a lover that finger paints me beautiful.

All I've ever learned comes down to this:
reality is a shaky ground,
but you can capture the sun,
lasso it's luminosity into a lava lamp,
turn today into the new year,
where a door wide enough
to walk through with open arms
has your name written on it,
and it opens up with a creak and a voice
of opportunity, cautioning,
yet welcoming a new beginning.

marry me

I remember when my father showed me a wrinkled worn-out postcard. On the front, a faded-to-yellow picture of a large wooden windmill sitting atop a luscious ice cream scoop shaped hill. On the back, a note written from my great-grandfather to my great-grandmother. Although I do not recall the exact wording, it read a little something like this:

> Darling,
> I'm certain that you'll leave me
> and fearful that you won't.
> There are troubled bubbles
> trapped in this ice,
> and I'm worried what might come out
> when I melt into you.
> A few fence posts used to mark
> the open field of my heart
> but over time they became
> wrapped in barbed wire,
> closing off, closing in,
> and here you are with wire cutters
> ready to set the cows free.
>
> Fortunately,
> I know what's good for me,
> and you, my dear,
> remind me of something
> I forgot a long time ago.
> Every time I look at my eyelids
> I think of you.
> Every golden word you say
> gets tucked next to the heart
> in my treasure chest.
>
> Sometimes I think the gods made us
> parallel lines and said never to meet.

Our parents certainly think so.
But I believe each generation must
break free of convention,
like the way the dawn broke
when you told me you love me.
I'll do whatever it takes for
us to be together,
even if that means building a whale
so we can live in its belly.
Lets furnish together.
You can call me Ishmael
and we'll fish for the stars.

flying free

I can't imagine putting love in a container for only one person.

It'd be like putting too many bees in a box
or too many birds in a cage.
I once fell in love for 30 seconds
with a women on the bus
because when she asked me where I got my pink scarf
with the silver tinsel threaded through it,
I felt like she was tinsel threading through my life
and when she hopped out the door
I had a little more sparkle in my step
than 30 seconds before.

And when the young boy in the grocery store
picked up a carrot, offered it to me,
and said, "It helps with night vision, you know.
To keep away the monsters and scary stuff,"
my heart melted into the floor so much
they needed a clean up in aisle 4,
because strangers to me have never been strange,
more like characters in a play
that simply need more show time to show how
much they truly shine.

Perhaps it is the clouds,
or the planes that fly through them,
or how I am so loving and
committed to the same sun
that turns the sunflowers
in its directions
and tethers the earth to its light,
but something makes this world full of
too many beautiful things
with which to fall in love with.

So many that my heart becomes scattered across the sky
making friends with the stars
lifting me nearer so that when I leave this earth,
people will know that if you try to explain love
you'll be left with plain love,
and love is riding the feeling
of the amateur astronomer looking
through her new telescope
discovering music and miracles
and birds flying free from their cages.

heading home

And I remember my mother said,
"*I know.*
You've been all over the world now,
and excited about your big job in the big city.
But just so you know,
in case things get too much,
or it doesn't work out,
or it gets too lonely,
know that,
there's always a room for you here,
there's always a room for you here."

So I went home.
For the first time in 10 years,
I went home.

Up the stairs
my room hadn't changed.
I gazed over the teddy bears, chess trophies,
Kurt Cobain posters and nostalgia,
and I remembered,

you.

And the way you blushed whenever I caught your eye.

So I called you up.
I know.
It's been a long time.
We were so young.
But we made each other's days.
We made love,
and we made mistakes.
We also made a melody,
one full of love notes that danced across the pages,

and the highs got so mixed in with the lows,
it became a symphony.

I remember in our final goodbye
off to college,
off to another life,
you pointed to your heart and said,
there's always a room for you here,
there's always a room for you here.

ups and downs

When I first saw a picture of the earth,
I thought: what a perfect circle we walk upon,
a *yin-yang* of land and water,
struggle and success.

Tonight is the solar eclipse,
where the moon and the sun become one in the sky,
it's beautiful,
but you mustn't look at it directly.

Sometimes I feel the same way about sorrow,
it's too hard to meet head on,
lest something inside gets destroyed,
but there's a trick to this one too.

The light is still there;
even the small fish at the bottom of the ocean
breathes oxygen,
and love is to be found anywhere.

I got mad love,
it drives me crazy the way
people lose track of their own hearts
and become homeless.

But heat rises,
and happiness floats,
and crystals form naturally,
and wishes do come true.

So come back into this light, this life,
dip your hands into the beach sand,
hike 10 miles just to see that one luminescent waterfall,
where the tadpoles grow in tiny pools.

Place both hands on your chest,
and feel,
the truth of it all:
we are blessed to be here.

one never knows

As a kid,
Adults would ask me questions I wouldn’t know the answer to.
Like,
what do you want to be when you grow up?

During those times,
I often put my hands in my pockets
and looked down at my shoes.
I pretended there was sand between my toes
stuck from my travels on Saturn.

Fortunately,
I kept The Little Prince in my pocket.
I took him out whenever I didn't know what to do.
Often he told me, "One never knows!"
And I would go, "Darn it, Peter,"
(I call him Peter)
"That doesn't help."

But I remember one time he said,
"My planet is so small.
if you run fast enough towards the sunset
you can make a moment last forever.
But your planet is large.
And a bit scary.
And despite so many people,
it can be incredibly lonely sometimes.

But you have a saying that I do enjoy,
'Reach for the stars,'
you say.
Don't let pesky thoughts limit what is possible."

Hmmm….
What do I want to be?

I want to be perfect and I want to be me.
I want to be the clouds and I want to be the wind that flows through them.

I want to be in a hot air balloon,
made out of frosting,
with a polka dotted elephant,
and all my best friends.
With a giant telescope that takes in not only the stars but sees all the way into people
that it sees the good in them,
sees the love in them,
sees the child in them.

Then maybe happily ever after wouldn't be such a fantasy.

correspondence

Dear universe,
I wish to move back in time,
I feel like I'm on borrowed life,
like neither this world nor this body is mine,
and especially not meant for me.
There is sorrow, betrayal, pain,
hidden in the corners,
in the street lamps,
in brick walls and alleyways.
The seasons wear down my skin,
so that I feel way too much.

Reply:
My sweet child,
I give you flowers but you see only stems.
I give you stars but you see only empty space.
Even the most gorgeous cerulean river has muddy banks.
Your concern for yourself and others reflects nothing but love.
For warriors like yourself,
it is better to be overly sensitive.
It helps one find the way,
the beauty in mystery,
and the soft center I placed at the heart of every living being.

one

Be fun, be playful,
be light, be divine.
Be joy, be laughter,
be love beyond time.

two

Let go, relax,
smile, just be.
Feel the rain,
feel the sun,
feel joy,
feel free.

three

Life is so beautiful,
beyond belief,
even through the sadness,
even through the grief,
people come,
people leave,
through it all,
love reigns supreme.

wide open

Can you imagine the feeling of being born?
Can you imagine opening your eyes for the first time,
what that would feel like?
Such amazement, wonder, awe.

It must be like that moment between sleeping and waking,
before dreams dissolve into this accidental universe,
when anything seems possible.

I think if we learn to pay attention again,
to notice what's happening right now and all around,
to hold that glass of water
like you just realized it is the source of all life,
we would feel very much the same.

so simple

I have something that makes me rich,
it puts everything at ease,
it makes the entire world,
seem to wait on me.

By a river in the forest,
I found it on my own,
dipping a finger into the water
peace chilled me to the bone.

It is the simple feeling,
I know it to be true,
that I am part of everything
and the whole is part of you.

drinking roses on sunday

Let the rain fall where it may,
there's a gentleness to life,
gentleladies, gentlemen and gentlequeers,
let it be.

Come over to my place,
I'm drinking roses this Sunday,
soaking up tea leaves,
letting Miles Davis' trumpet combine intimacy and ambience.
Although we may lay in the grass on blankets of silver linings
and laugh at the sky,
share poetry, song and story,
this is not a lazy Sunday.
Comets appear stationary.
While we are hurtling through space at a million miles an hour,
we are conclusive evidence
that happiness is not something you pursue,
it's something you make.

I'm selling rainbows this Sunday
One for a secret.
Buy three get a free kiss.

opening night

I love love. I really do.
I love how it sprinkles happiness on my shoulders
how it warms the chicken soup in my soul.

I love these bodies and everything they have to offer.
I love how they lose themselves in each other,
get tangled up the way two galaxies meet
and intertwine after a few billion years.

So come over tonight.
I'm inviting friendly lovers and lovely friends.
It's opening night,
with open hearts and open minds open to possibility.
Where we dine with destiny,
discover closeness, kindness, caring,
and laugh in the face of death.

Of course,
love is the entree,
As well as the dessert.
Food for the soul if I've ever said so.

Here's how it goes:
Ask the questions that scare you the most
like,
am I on the right path?
What am I doing with my life?
Am I as smart/kind/loving/pretty/lucky/happy as I think I am?
What if she doesn't really love me?

Take those thoughts and supposed answers that bubble up,
(Notice how you can fit 'em into a thimble)
(Even so, there's no room for them here)
stuff them into a stick of dynamite
and toss that into an active volcano.

Today's mantra is
let go into love
let go into love
let go into love
let go into love

If you keep going,
you'll find the YOU you've been looking for.

they say our love is

They say our love is like in the movies,
where the odds of us not meeting were so great,
God must not have had anything better to do,
and everybody watching can't help but smile 'cuz,
they want to believe that dreams come true.

They say our love is like the ocean,
and worry disappears on the horizon like sailboats,
and all those waves we're going through,
don't mask the depth, that floating feeling,
and how through it all the water carries you.

But I say our love is like a butterfly,
finding sweetness in the smallest of places,
beautiful and gentle with wings covered in morning dew,
open to the perpetual change of life,
allowing the heart to fly wherever it wants to.

i am

I am.
That much I know for sure.

I would say I am living,
or
I am a human being,
but to be honest,
I don't know the true meaning of either.

But I do know that *I am.*

I am a son, a brother, a partner, friend, a lover,
a part-time chef, an aspiring yogi, a pretend poet, a lazy writer,

a shoulder to cry on,
an open heart,
a helping hand,
a listening ear,
an occasional philosopher
and an occasional fuck-up.

I am a floating pattern of
light and energy,
song and dance,
tears and laughter.

I am both all of these
and none of them at the same time.
For to define is to limit,
and I believe we are all limitless beings,
capable of anything and everything and lifetimes of love.

It's a shame the heart doesn't recognize how beautiful it truly is.

bask

If you unabashedly
open your heart,
like the full moon in the night,
suddenly,
every malnourished cell in your body,
is cleansed in glorious light.

Be brazen,
young lover,
take no prisoners,
dance out loud,
scream and shout.

Life doesn't wait,
but it's always there
for those courageous enough
to let go first.

warning: fragile

Spirits caught for a moment
in the net of time and space,
as formless becomes form,
so comes the human race.

Shaped like oceans
dipped in laughter,
we flap our wings just once,
and it feels like forever.

Life is a gift
beyond compare,
we must unwrap it with love,
open with care.

stay strong

If you want to hold the weight of the world,
and love every living being,
you have to open you heart just as much.
You can't pick and choose.

If you reject somebody,
push somebody away,
hold grudges too tightly against the cold,
you're holding off parts of yourself.

So love yourself first,
love yourself completely.
Accept all the parts,
even the bad ones.

Then love everyone,
love everyone completely.
Accept everyone,
you'll find there are no bad ones.

paradise

I was black coffee and your silky skin was a milky cream
that swirled through my world until I too could taste sweetness.
So I bought us an Italian sailboat with a funny name,
and we let the wind take us to where heaven touches the earth.

We spend all our lives floating through spectra.
The light of the moon, the light of the sea,
the sight of your silhouette next to me,
waves of bird calls and water ripples and heartbeats
and everything that's ever existed.

Artists imagine condensing such beauty of life into a painting,
maybe even a masterpiece called *chaotic bliss*,
but we are knee deep it in, my love,
opening presents of promise, kindness, sunflowers
and everything that's ever existed.

once upon a time

We were once children,
finding awe in our pockets,
wonder underneath clover leaves,
and every touch was like magic.

We were once planets,
that flew through the comets,
where the stars pierced like needles,
the rings of Saturn were our targets.

We were once spirals,
green, yellow, golden,
expanding through the aurora borealis,
tasting the salt of seashells.

I want to be like the light,
sliding across the forest canopy,
kissing your lips in the morning,
melting frost across prairies.

Remember the day you fell in love with a mermaid,
with blue eyes as deep as oceans,
you flew through the fog,
like swans as soft as silk.

Let us grow diamonds in our hearts,
keep safe what we hold dear,
hug a ladybug,
and dance through our fears.

both

Truth or dare?

Truth.
Of course.
Honesty.
Nothing I value more than honesty.

On the other hand,
dare.
Because I dare you to live,
to do the things that scare you most.

My friend says that I'm a Sagittarius.
and my tombstone is going to say "What's next?"
Cuz I want it all.

So how about,
heads and tails,
truth and dare,
trick and treat.
Are you top or bottom? Switch.
Male or female? Yes please.

I'm polyamorous too.
It works out better this way.
It works out better that way too.

my school

When I go to school,
I want to major in love,
minor in compassion,
study the heart,
and learn how to live.

Why is that so hard,
surely I'm not the only one,
perhaps you too.

In my school,
love rules.
In my school,
we dance,
we play.
In my school,
emotions are not to be pushed away
but cared for every day.
In my school gratitude is grown,
compassion is cultivated,
empathy is emphasized.

In my school there is discipline,
discipline in not turning away,
facing suffering,
and helping those in need.

Why don't they teach us this in school?
Teach us how to become lovers,
to become friends,
teach me to understand,
teach us to dream.
Do you remember how to dream?

such is life

I woke up last night
in pure terror
from an already-forgotten dream.
My trembling hands filled a glass of water half empty,
three melatonins and one dramamine later,
gravity tripled in strength,
my mind let go,
and I remembered what it is like to die.

I woke up today
to find the sunlight passing through the window
at just the right angle
so that its rays refracted across the half full glass of water,
creating an ocean of rainbows on my ceiling
and I remembered what it was like to be born.

feel that?

Love gets me up in the morning,
an almost intrusive alarm clock of wind chimes and ocean
waves,
as morning awe and wonder cascade through the window.

The way to heaven is one of astonishment,
like a toy boat floating through
the peace of the babbling brook.

Try to be good,
and believe in good,
but more importantly forgive yourself when you don’t do either.

You feel,
therefore you are more than what you see in the mirror,
more beauty and depth than a fractal flower.

Our spirits are always traveling sunward,
bringing warmth to the cold and light to the dark.
Life is simply remembering to be here now,

discovering the possibilities in somehow,
letting be, letting go,
letting in.

Like a tea candle strapped to a paper bag,
saying yes,
lift me, lift me nearer.

the earth without art

Over dinner she says,
sometimes you act like you're 12.

Well,
sometimes I feel like I'm 12,
except with a handlebar mustache.
Let me finish my milk first,
then cuddles,
in a blanket fort.

And as a matter of fact yes,
I was picturing myself,
chopping up an apple and putting it back to together,
this time with a little note inside
containing a few measures of jazz music.
So when the doctor says an apple a day,
I'll know he means,
be sure to dance and sing,
create art in everything.
Do life and do it in the best way possible,
live as though all you know are mysteries.

They say we have only explored 5% of the world's oceans,
if you go to great depths with even greater courage,
you'll discover a story worth telling,
one unseen by the naked eye.

nothing is lost

Years ago, I remember
when she lost her virginity.
She cried.

She said,
Why does beauty have to end?
Why does it seem like a runaway train
is always coming around the bend?
Why is my sweater always unraveling?
Why is the sand always flowing through these fingers?
Why am I so fucking tired all the time?
These aches these pains,
these bad days and sad ways.
Will you keep my heart safe?

But…
I said,
You're like,
you're like avocados and quinoa.
You're like presents when it's not even my birthday,
like a hand plunging into the water when I can't swim,
like the man on the moon and the lady in the water
fell in love in a field of flowers and made you,
blowing dandelion kisses across mountains.

You flipped my world upside down,
so that the ocean became the sky full of star fish,
curing my jellyfish stings with dolphin kisses,
and the rain turned so salty I'm not sure
if those are tears or raindrops.

We all have known the despair of failure,
been bruised behind our backs,
spent most of our lives trying to keep it together.
There is always tomorrow.

and tomorrow there will be a tomorrow.
Nothing ever repeats itself,
which means things end all too often
but there is absolutely nothing more special than you
in this moment right now.

sometimes

All I can say is,
sometimes beauty sends shivers up my spine.
Sometimes these atoms of mine dissolve into wonder,
the way the horizon dissolves into color.

Sometimes there are birds in my chest,
sometimes they struggle to get out,
sometimes my heart cracks open
so much my ribcage bursts

and they all fly up up up and away,
finding space to breathe,
space to sing,
space to soar above everything.

I can't help but let the world wash over me.
I can't help but feel the love deep inside.
My mind goes on forever, it seems.
I get lost in my own dreams sometimes.

I want magic and I want it to be real.
I want dragon's teeth and to be in Salvador Dali's art class.
I want the pain of this body to melt away
into a beam of light blue light.

I want the crashing cymbal and the sound of Beethoven's piano
and to kiss Mona Lisa's smile.
I want to brush away that one strand of hair curling into your soft
lips,
gaze into your eyes and dive deep into love.

be free

Stay present,
be present,
enjoy your present.

Open to love,
fall in love,
spread your love.

Listen, receive,
Let go, release,
soften, ease,
slowly, breathe,
give, please.

Not knowing,
keep going.

Kiss, rise,
lick, slide,
touch, tickles,
nipples, nibbles.

Be free of what you are for now,
there will be another day,
for everything else.

This moment,
so simple,
drop in.

"I am complete."

more than one reality

Coffee tables.
Yes, coffee tables.
A termite's food.
A carpenter's project.
An artist's masterpiece.
A resting place for books no one reads.
And a platform for my feet today.
But tonight in the dark it will become my big toe's worst enemy.
Life is what you make it.

Meanwhile,
I'm here,
roof over my head, serenaded by raindrops and thunder.
The mood is set for poetry and wine.
Looking outside the window,
a woman in the street
ducks for cover underneath an awning,
clutching a purse above her ahead and cursing the weather.
A store owner scrambles to cover his fruits.
A smiling child jumps from puddle to puddle.
And red robins hop hop hop around
looking for worms pushed up by the flooding of their
underground homes.

There is one world, of course,
of which we are all members.
But we all perceive it differently,
we make our own reality.
Do you see the beauty, behind it all?
It's there.
Look through your heart,
for a change,
see the love,
it's there too.

peace

Like a stone smoothed by water,
maybe peace is the natural state of things.
Such little things it takes
for thoughts to lay
to rest like floating petals in a warm breeze.
No words,
just notice,
the enterprising ant crawling next to you,
the pleasure of the first kiss,
the sound of footsteps on a long and winding gravel road
through a luscious and precious forest,
and the trees giving each other space.

With a few sunflower seeds,
a bluebird will come to eat from your outstretched hands.
All life asks for is a bit of patience and understanding.

A simple stick tossed into a moving creek,
will see far more than you or I.
Let go of the banks and just imagine a voice saying,
this!
And this and this,
this is air,
this is water,
this is the breath.
Can you believe it?
That you're here for it?
This the only planet in the universe
with flowers,
with bees,
with honey, with nectar,
(so sweet and so simple)
and this enterprising ant
holding a sense of purpose
as delicate as your own.

don't worry

There is poetry in the corners,
untold stories in the rafters,
spirits in between the window panes,
mysteries in your morning cup of coffee,
entire universes of glory abound but
they are squeezed and stripped
and robbed of ecstasy and wonder
and all your mind is left with is
constancy, constancy, constancy.

But you are an expression of the universe and
the universe is an expression of God's love:
a continual state of creation,
becoming,
becoming,
becoming.

So don't worry,
no one really dies.
If you're here right now
you'll be here then too.

how *drinking roses on sunday* came to be

Maybe you walk down the same street everyday on the way to work, but this one morning in March after too many weeks of rain, the clouds decide they are finished crying. The world is still damp with that glorious after-rain smell and you keep your head down and your hands in your pockets as you walk, until you almost step on this worm trying to make its way across the sidewalk.

So it stops you. And you look up, for the first time noticing what is around you, like the pitter-pattering of raindrops falling off bare branches. The pattern the sleeping grass makes in the mud. The warm and cozy houses that keep everyone warm and cozy. How your sweater makes your torso too hot but your nose is cold and turning pink. Suddenly it occurs to you that life is one big poem; that's the way things are and that's the way they will always be. So this feeling in this moment pulls a few words out of you and you try to make note of them.

But the words compared to the surreality of it all feel more like a prison than perfection. So you wait for that thing to happen again just the way it did so maybe it gives you a few more words to go along with what you've got. Then you realize it was the too-specific series of circumstances, including the mundane road and the weeks of rain dissolving the corpse of winter and how you would not have even looked up if it weren't for that one particular worm crossing the sidewalk at that one particular moment.

So instead, you take matters into your own hands with a laptop and cup of tea, close your eyes and write and write and write. You write unforgivingly, impetuously, wildly, like it's the last and only words you'll ever say to an 8-year-old boy who desperately wants wonder to last forever.

You confess all your life experiences, like your first kiss and getting drunk after high school graduation and attending the funeral of your best friend and all the places your mind goes when it wanders. Then you take them distill out everything unnecessary until an essential oil with your fingerprints, your blood and your truth comes out; and it tastes and smells a bit like heaven.

It’s a long process and it’s not easy. Maybe there’s a better way, but I haven’t found it yet.

So that is my advice: keep an eye out for the worms in your life.

And good luck.

about the author

Zach has spent much of his adult life trying to connect love to the stars. Most of the time this meant shedding layers upon layers of hard scaly skin until the raw vulnerabilities of the heart came to the surface, but sometimes it involved rearranging words in the dictionary until some semblance of allure and fascination began to formulize.

And just as an idea grows on you like a vine across a Cathedral's colored windows, this young man began to have delusions of himself as a poet.

Despite the specters of insecurity and self-judgment, he managed to squeeze his brain like a lemon until the juice of a few poems came out. Once finished, he thought to himself, "Like cough syrup, this may not be any good. But it may help someone, somewhere, feel a little bit better."

Made in the USA
San Bernardino, CA
09 August 2014